These Things I Love

Stillman J. Elwell

Also by the author:

Windows of Thought

These Things I Love

by Stillman J. Elwell

Illustrations by Diane Orchard

The Naylor Company
Book Publishers of the Southwest
San Antonio, Texas

Library of Congress Cataloging in Publication Data

Elwell, Stillman J.
These things I love.

Poems.
I. Title.
PS3509.L86T5 811'.5'2 75-43779
ISBN 0-8111-0610-1

Printed in the United States of America

To Mary

Whose devotion and help have made this book possible.

Contents

These Things I Love

These things I love – the silent hills,
The magic of the last faint ray
That lingers when the sun goes down
To glorify the dying day;
The breath of spring, the fleecy clouds,
The silver moon that rides on high,
The great gray geese that wing their way
Across the late October sky.

These too, I love – the broad green fields
That turn with passing time to gold,
The hush that settles in the pines
When snow is deep and nights are cold,
The year, that when its work is done
Puts on the scarlet robes of fall,
The still cold stars of winter's night,
And that Great Hand that guides them all!

The Snows of Time

Farther and farther and farther away
Are the rides we took in the open sleigh,
Faintly more faintly the sound of the bells
Over the crest of the hill-range swells.

Deeper and deeper Time's drifted snow
Covers the scenes of the long ago,
Covers the sleigh tracks long and white
That stretched away in the moonlit night;

Covers the fields and the woodlots, too,
Just as the old snows used to do,
Till the friends we loved and the sleighbells' chime
Seem buried deep in the Snows of Time!

But the old snows vanished when springtime came,
And the Snows of Time will do just the same,
If you'll leave the present and come with me
Down the long, long road of the "Used To Be!"

For there alone do the old friends sing,
And only there do the sleighbells ring,
And no where else, on a moonlit night,
Do the sleigh-tracks glisten long and white!

Wealthy

I've seen hard times along the way
And felt the hand of debt,
By many standards, I suppose
I'd be called poor – And yet . . .

My wife and I go down the lane
When evening sun is low,
The shadows climb the eastern hills,
The west is all aglow.

The dog goes racing on ahead,
The cats are just behind,
They seem to tell us in their way
How well they like our kind.

We stand beneath the giant pines
And hear their whispered song,
Unheard by those whose ears are tuned
To voices of the throng!

We see the splendor of the skies,
The heaven's awesome span,
And somehow I can't help but feel
That I'm a wealthy man!

Complaints

I complained my feet were hurting
In a voice that spoke of doom,
But I walked across the meadow
When the clover was in bloom;
And I roamed in autumn woodlands
In a blaze of gold and brown,
And I climbed the hill at evening
Just to watch the sun go down!

I was sorry that my hearing
Wasn't what it ought to be,
Wasn't quite as keen as others',
Or it seemed that way to me.
But I stood in awe and wonder
When the harmony sublime
Of the anthems of the ages
Filled the air at Christmas Time!

I complained of seeing poorly,
"Glasses should be changed," I thought,
"I can't read as many pages
As it seems to me I ought!
Faulty vision is a menace,
What with all my other ills!"
Yet I saw the purple glory
Of the Everlasting Hills!

October

There's a magic in October
Like no other time of year,
There's a touch of melancholy
And a bit of solemn cheer.

Memories come back before us
That had seemed forgotten long,
But are now as bright as noonday,
Like a well remembered song!

Other days and other seasons
Have a certain charm well known,
But a day in bright October
Has a magic all its own.

Then it is, all earth turns crimson,
Red and yellow, gold and brown,
With a touch of purple shadow
As the sun is going down.

Then be ready for the moment,
For the Clock of Time seems still
As you catch a glimpse of glory
Just beyond the western hill!

A Prayer

Great God of all the battlefields,
And of the ways of peace,
Stretch forth Thy hand and speak the word
That bids the tumult cease!

Let not the children of Thy love
Fan hatred into flame;
O, purge their souls of all desire
To hate and kill and maim!

On this, Thy footstool, let there come
A gladder brighter dawn,
Lest all the wisdom of the years
Be forfeited and gone!

Break forth the clouds that now obscure
The sun and stars above,
Take bitter madness from their hearts
And teach Thy children Love!

Leaving Home

I've often thought I'd leave the country home
And seek my fortune in the haunts of men,
Perhaps I'd even sail across the foam
In search of riches and of fame – But when?

I couldn't leave when first the flowers bloom,
And buds are bursting in the willow trees,
When spring awakens from its winter's tomb,
And robin's song is borne on every breeze.

'Twould break my heart when grain is waving tall,
And fields have turned from emerald to gold,
When meadows ring with bobwhite's cheery call,
And summer's all too fleeting joys are told.

And could I go when wood and hill and dale
Have donned their robes of crimson to proclaim
That, tho' the plans of man may change and fail,
The plan of Time is evermore the same?

Then, when the merry bells of Christmas ring
And moonbeams glisten on the drifted snow,
As good old friends the great glad carols sing,
Ah! Then I'm sure I cannot ever go!

The Load of Hay

I wondered why my Dad would choose
To walk behind the load of hay,
Instead of climbing up to ride
Beside me, on that long gone day.

He said the wagon jarred too much
When going over bumps and stones,
Such rides, he thought, were not for men
With swollen joints and aching bones!

Of course, I knew the lane was rough,
But little did it mean to me,
I couldn't know that all too soon,
As Dad was then, I too would be!

The scene persists, and through the years
A wistful thought comes back to mind,
I'd like to drive the team once more
If, somehow, Dad could walk behind!

Spring

Once again we've been reminded
Of the miracle of spring,
Once again the snows have melted
And again the robins sing.

Frogs sing gaily in the marshes,
And the trees their message tell
Of the age-old joy of springtime
As the buds begin to swell.

For there's something in the springtime
That is young and gay and fair,
As the earth and skies awaken
To the magic in the air!

It's a time of joy and promise,
Of fulfillment in good time,
Just as autumn brings its message
Of fulfillment more sublime.

For it seems that nature crowded
All the glory Time could bring,
All the wonders of the ages,
In these few short weeks of spring!

The World of Pine

O, come with me for a little while
To a faraway world I knew,
To a land of rollways and swollen streams
In the home of the logging crew;
For I was born in a world of pine
In a land of the axe and saw,
Where logs were gold and the hard raw edge
Of the hobnailed boots was law!

But now I live in a world of steel
Where men, like the eagles, soar —
Where skies above me and seas below
Resound to the motor's roar.
Don't feel secure in the world you know,
For soon it will be as mine —
A fabled part of a storied past,
As now is the world of pine!

September's Crossroads

When at last the summer's ended
And it's not quite time for fall,
Come a few short days of splendor
That are not of Time at all!

For they're not of any season,
These few magic golden days,
When the first faint glow of autumn
Tints the dying summer's haze.

Over Earth there comes the glory
Of a mighty solemn change,
For the year is at the crossroads
And the world seems new and strange!

Time itself is awed and pauses,
So it seems, its banners furled,
As it views this one brief moment
From another grander world!

The Silver Wedding

Years of youth are ever troubled,
And the years of age are dim,
Even tho' they wear the halo
Of a grand old evening hymn.

And the years of greatest service
Are the ones along the way,
So tonight we pause in honor
Of a Silver Wedding Day.

For the Silver Wedding's glory
Isn't youth and isn't age;
Then it is life's book is opened
At about the middle page.

And it's then we see the folly
Of our youthful doubts and fears,
Even as our days are strengthened
With the wisdom of the years.

Only then we know the glories
Of a youth that swiftly fled,
And the richer, deeper meaning
Of the years that lie ahead.

There are many glad occasions,
Many times our lives are blest,
But, perhaps, the Silver Wedding
Is, of all, the very best!

Old Dog Squeaker

Squeaker, I suppose you'll tell me
Was a dog as all dogs go,
Just an ordinary mongrel,
But, of course, you couldn't know,
For you see you never saw her
In her carefree younger days –
Fat as any ball of butter,
Brimming full of puppy ways.

And you had no way of knowing
Our Old Squeaker talked so well,
For you'd never read the message
Those brown eyes could plainly tell;
'Twas a message, when translated,
Said, "I love you – Not in part,
But with all my very being,
From the bottom of my heart!"

And, of course, you couldn't see her
In the little grave I'd dug,
Down the lane she loved to travel –
Couldn't feel the mighty tug
At my heartstrings as I shoveled,
Patting down the earth just so,
Or you'd never tell me Squeaker
Was a dog as all dogs go!

Old Jake

The neighbors smile as Old Jake hauls his load,
A load made lighter now that he is old;
They chuckle when they see him on the road
And wonder why he hasn't long been sold.

But I recall when Jake walked with his mate –
The proudest team in all the countryside,
Nor let his prancing footsteps e'er be late –
'Twas ever thus till good old Jerry died!

And Dad oft held the lines those bygone days,
As proud of them as they were prideful then;
But now I'm left alone to sing their praise,
For Dad, long since, has gone the way of men.

So now when Jake is old he needn't fear
That he must heed a stranger's voice unknown,
The dreaded trader or the auctioneer –
Old Jake will have a stall to call his own!

Kindly Words

It's kindly words that build this life,
And make it worth the living;
Both they who give and who receive
Are better for the giving.

They cost so little, mean so much,
Such thorny pathways soften,
That no one understands just why
They aren't used more often.

Far more than gold or precious stones
Their memory is treasured,
For by another set of rules
Their sterling worth is measured.

For wealth departs and flowers fade,
And golden threads may sever,
But kindly words of friendly souls
Live in the heart forever!

His Presence

I cannot know — much less explain,
The wonders of the hand
That guides the planets through the night,
And rules the sea and land;
For who am I to tell of One
The sun and moon obey,
Who knows and rules the countless stars
That line the Milky Way?

I know but this — when in the west
The sun is sinking low,
And on the far-flung purple hills
There falls a last faint glow,
When from the church across the lea
The evening bell I hear,
There comes a feeling in my soul
That He is very near!

The Vanished Pine

I would tell of a town in the forest dark,
Where the murmuring pines soughed low,
And the marvelous deeds of the lumberjacks
In the days of the long ago;
Of the ring of the axe on the frosty air
And the crash of the falling pine,
And the scream of the saws in the roaring mills
In that long ago home of mine.

I would tell of the bells on the loggers' teams,
And I'd boast of the rollways high,
But I wouldn't recall that the sad day came
When it all had to fade and die.
No, I wouldn't relate that the mills are gone,
And the pines and the loggers too;
There'd be never a word of that sorry fact,
But alas, and alack – It's true!

A Helping Hand

If no one worked for anything but money,
Nor strove for anything but sordid gain,
I wonder would this good old world be sunny,
Or would we search for happiness in vain?

Would anyone in such a world spend hours
In giving comfort to a friend in need?
Would gardens be abloom with fragrant flowers,
If cash alone were everybody's creed?

Would any little childish hands be lifted
To those who stronger, wiser were than they?
And who would stoop to help a friend less gifted,
Or plant his feet more firmly on the way?

If no one worked without a profit showing,
And not a thing in all this life was free,
There wouldn't be a single rosebud growing —
And what a sorry place this world would be!

Perspective

Two men are walking down the street –
One sees the dust that's at his feet;
The other's eyes are on the hills,
And to their spell his spirit thrills.

The distant slope, the setting sun,
Enthrall the soul of only one,
For he who fails to lift his eyes
Sees not the glory of the skies!

Tho' both must walk the selfsame way,
Perform the selfsame tasks each day,
One never looks beyond the clod,
The other sees the hills – and God!

Johnny Appleseed

Just o'er the hill there stands a house
With roof and doors caved in,
A crumbled wall of mossy stones
Tells where a barn has been;
Nearby there bravely blossoms still
A gnarled old apple tree,
A monument to one whose fame
Has spread from sea to sea.

He traveled long and weary miles
With little thought of pay,
He knew the hardship and the toil
So common in his day;
His task? To see that men who lived
Long after his brief time,
Might see the blossoms, taste the fruit,
Of his own native clime.

So when you tell of dauntless men
Who made this nation great,
Who laid foundations firm and deep
And fashioned well her fate,
Who gave their all, and not in vain,
To serve their country's need –
Just save a high and honored place
For Johnny Appleseed!

My Neighbor

My neighbor's ways are not as mine,
They irritate and grieve me,
And often he's so out of line
I almost wish he'd leave me.

I know he thinks I'm crazy too,
There's not a chance to doubt it,
I don't know how to live, it's true,
The way he feels about it.

But when I'm sick or something's wrong
Like cattle in the clover,
And I can't seem to get along,
He says, "I'll be right over."

He's always here to lend a hand
When sorrow overtakes me;
He never fails to understand
When Fortune's smile forsakes me.

And so, of all the folks I know
Who praise, disdain or cheer me,
I'll let the others come and go,
But keep my neighbor near me!

At the Hospital

Long rows of rooms on either side,
A long, long aisle between,
Where now and then a woman walks,
And now and then – a queen;
They're dressed in white, and some with caps,
And some with frocks of blue,
I think it has to do with rank,
Or kinds of work they do.

We laymen have a better way
To tell what rank they hold,
It doesn't have to do with dress
Or caps or braids of gold,
But, rather, with a kindly face,
A word, a touch, a smile,
For now and then an angel walks
Along that long, long aisle!

A Song

Sometimes people try to tell you
That a song is just a song –
Other things are more important
As this Old World rolls along –
But I've seen men gather riches,
Climb the rugged heights of fame,
Yes, and go in bitter sorrow
To the lowest depths of shame!

But their riches often failed them
With the passing of the years,
And the fame for which they'd struggled
Brought them only grief and tears;
Still their spirits could be lifted
And their faith be made more strong
By the magic spell of music
And the miracle of song.

So I've come to know – there's nothing
Stirs the human heart and soul
Like a song that tells the story
Of a never dying goal;
And that nothing quite so surely
Spans the chasm deep that lies
Just between us and the glory
Of that land beyond the skies!

Dad's Concern

I remember a little barefoot lad
In the far-off long ago,
And a tall lean man with a long moustache
Who was working with a hoe;
'Twas a sultry day and the fields lay parched
In the blazing summer sun,
And 'twas much too hot in the burning sand
For the feet of the little one.

So the man would dig to the cool moist soil,
And the boy would come and stand
In sheer delight in the good brown earth,
All safe from the burning sand;
But the sun worked fast and 'twould not be long
Till the boy would again complain,
And the man would dig as he'd done before
Till those feet could be cooled again!

It is all so clear, though the years are long,
I remember it well you see,
For the tall lean man with the hoe was Dad,
And the barefoot boy was me!
And I have learned as I've gone through life,
Through the storm, and the cold, and heat,
How few are concerned as was dear old Dad,
With the fate of my wayward feet!

Mighty World

Oh! Let me live in a mighty world
Where the raging storms o'er the mountains sweep,
Where the ice is thick at the river's brim
And the pale stars glitter when snow is deep;
In a world of thunder and lightning flash,
Of trackless forest and lake and stream,
Where a man is dwarfed by the works of God,
And is lost, unnoticed, in Time's great scheme!

Yes, let me live in a lovely world,
Where the spring's green carpet is summer's gold,
Where the hills and hedges are bursts of flame
When the summer wanes and the year is old;
And lovely still when the flame is gone
And the great gray geese with their strident call
Proclaim once more in their own sure way
That the God of Nature is over all!

But never, Oh! Never let me live
In that little world of another kind,
Hemmed in by the walls of a narrow room,
And the stronger walls of a narrow mind –
A mind that searches for fancied wrongs,
Nor sees the grandeur of Earth and Sky –
May I not retreat to that little world
And Miss the Glories that Pass me By!

Sons

I have no son but this I know,
Each little bright-eyed lad
Believes no other man on earth
Is equal to his dad;
He likes to do the things he does
And follow where he goes,
He's filled with questions, for you see
He's sure his daddy knows!

Alas! This time is all too short,
For when he's taller grown
He wouldn't waste his time to learn
The things his dad has known;
He'd rather figure for himself
Whatever comes along,
He's very certain he is right
And that his dad is wrong!

But this impresses me the most
Of all the things I've learned
About the changing ways of sons;
When Life has downward turned,
And they, in turn, have felt the touch
Of Time's fast-drifting snow,
They never cease to tell the things
That "Dad Said Long Ago!"

My Choice

Now some may travel the wide world o'er,
And sail on the stormy seas,
Their anchors cast on a foreign shore,
Their sails in a foreign breeze,
May love to study the works of art
By the masters of brush or pen,
Yet fail to learn from that mighty chart
Not made by the hands of men!

So let them climb to the lofty heights
And knock at the door of fame,
Their lives be drawn to the gleaming lights
As moths to the deadly flame,
And let them glorify, if they will,
The scepter and robe and crown,
But let me stand on a high old hill,
And watch while the sun goes down!

Farms and Kingdoms

I remember, I remember,
Just as well as anything,
When a farmstead was a kingdom
And a farmer was a king;
Apples grew in every orchard,
And without a bit of spray,
And the granaries were bulging,
And the barns were full of hay.

I remember winter evenings,
After supper and the chores,
When the raging winds were howling
In the blizzard out of doors,
How we sat around the heater,
Felt its magic snug and warm,
Eating popcorn – all unmindful
Of the fury of the storm!

No one yet has made a picture
(And I'm sure they never will)
Like a wheatfield – tall and waving –
Or a meadow on a hill;
Like a cornfield in October
With its shocks in endless rows,
Or a woodlot stark and silent,
Fast asleep in winter snows!

No, we didn't have much money
And the days were hard and long,
But we had the things we needed
And we finished with a song;
And I'm certain you'll forgive me
If to those old days I cling,
When a farmstead was a kingdom
And a farmer was a king!

I Wonder

Yes, the lilacs are in blossom
Just the way they used to be,
And the fence is there as always
Right beside the old oak tree.

And the path winds down the hillside
Just the way it used to wind,
Though it's overgrown with brambles
And is harder now to find.

So it's much the same as always
In the springtime of the year,
All except it seems so lonely
Where it once was filled with cheer.

And I wonder – Can you tell me
Of a sound I used to know,
Coming through the woods at twilight
Like an echo, soft and low?

When the shadows fill the valley
Do you hear the plaintive song
Of the whippoorwill still calling,
Where the old house stood so long?

Little Things

As you gaze upon the mountain,
Don't forget the little hill;
As there's glory in the fountain,
So there's beauty in the rill.

Is the gale with all its power
Greater than the evening breeze,
Or the gentle summer shower
With its patter in the trees?

Just the faintest ray of gladness
Penetrates the deepest gloom,
Lighting up a world of sadness
As a candle lights a room.

And the story of the ages,
That the Hands of Time unlock,
Writes itself on tiny pages
Known as seconds, on the clock!

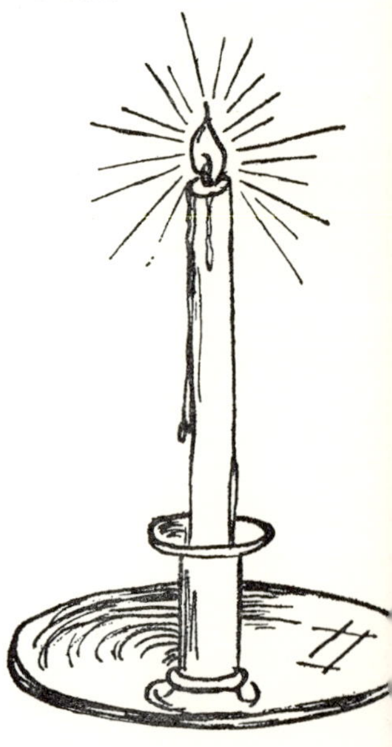

Participation

You have seen the home team battle
With a runner on each base,
And have felt the hush that settles
As the batter takes his place;
Seen the fielder's hopeless racing
For a hit that scored them all –
But you couldn't feel the triumph
Of the man who hit the ball!

You have heard a song come pouring
From a gifted singer's throat,
And have marvelled at the beauty
Of each lovely lilting note;
You have listened there enraptured,
Felt the tenseness of the throng –
But you couldn't know the glory
Of the singer of the song.

So it is with any pleasure,
Work or play that you may name,
Be it life's most pressing problem
Or the simplest childhood game;
If you'd know the joy of living,
Happy be, and glad and proud,
You'll just have to be a "doer,"
Not a watcher in the crowd!

A Reminder

Once again the great gray honkers
Sound their loud triumphant cry,
Once again their chains are lifted
To the gray November sky.

High above a world of sorrow,
Swift, unerring, day or night,
Monarchs of the autumn heavens
In the majesty of flight.

Over wilderness and city,
Village, farm and wooded glen,
Ever onward, all unmindful
Of the puny works of men.

And I wonder as I watch them
Pierce the sky on tireless wings,
Why it is we think we're greatest
In the mighty scheme of things.

For it seems that God has brought them
From their frozen homes afar
As a beacon to remind us
Just how very small we are!

Fancies

O dream, if you must, of the towering steep
On the heights as they meet the sky,
Of the nameless terror that haunts the deep
When the raging waves roll high.
But I shall pause and my heart will thrill
To dream as the sun sinks low,
Of an old white school on an old low hill
In the days of the long ago.

Yes, dream if you will of the glittering gold
In the palaces of state,
Of the wealth and power its masters hold
Hemmed in by the walls of hate!
But let me dream in the deepening gloam,
And my wayward fancy stray
To the friends I loved as we trudged back home
From school at the close of day!

Distance

I climbed the heights to the mountain's peak,
'Twas rugged and gray and bare;
I thought, "Good folk who would beauty seek
Must search for its charm elsewhere."

And then I turned in the fading glow
That comes with the setting sun,
Retraced my steps to the valley low
To rest, for the day was done.

Behold, my mountain was gorgeous now,
With purple and rose and gold,
The twilight magic had touched its brow
With beauty and grace untold.

O, purple distance, O, sunset ray,
O, mountain so bleak and lone,
Your glory comes with the dying day,
'Tis then you ascend your throne.

There is a mountain we know as Life,
It's thorny and hard and steep,
Its smoothest pathways are crossed with strife,
Its caverns are sheer and deep.

And there's a sunset that comes with age,
A distance of passing time,
Their glory that of the finished page,
Their grandeur – A faith sublime!

The Book of Life

Now, you may read from the greatest minds
That have lived in any age,
May study hard in a thousand books –
And forget each shining page.

But after all, does it matter much?
For the pages may be turned –
Review will bring you the knowledge lost
By the lessons poorly learned.

But there's a book called "The Book of Life,"
And the pages turn one way;
There's no review and there's no retreat –
They are turning day by day.

Then read your books as the years go by,
And forget them all when done,
And careless be, if it suits your taste,
In your studies – All save one!

But study well in "The Book of Life,"
Learn its precepts, come what may,
And give each lesson your very best –
For the pages turn one way!

Sixty Years

Perhaps no other sixty years
In all the ages past,
Have brought such mingled tragedy
And triumph as the last!

The heavy hobnailed boots of Mars
Have left their trail of woe;
At times the lights of all mankind
Have flickered, dim and low!

But through it all the mind of man
Has delved in nature's store
To find a better way of life
Than he had known before.

And yet, today, I do not care
To tell of war and strife,
Nor of the change the scientists
Have wrought in human life.

I'd rather tell of simple things
That haven't changed at all –
The great green carpet of the spring,
The scarlet robes of fall!

I'd try to wield that matchless brush,
The slowly setting sun,
And paint the purple on the hills
When day, at last, is done!

I'd tell you of the quiet love
Of one friend for another,
And speak the words that touch your hearts,
Like "Home and Dad and Mother!"

For there are things that go their way
Untouched by passing time –
The truth, the grandeur of the hills,
The noble, the sublime!

Our Country

Down the pleasant valleys,
Down the winding streams,
Up the rugged mountains
Rode the men of dreams;
Westward, ever westward
On the wings of fate,
From the Rock at Plymouth
To the Golden Gate.

Here they cross a river,
There they build a town,
Carving field and farmland
From the forest brown;
Blazing trails and pathways
Toward horizons blue —
These were men of vision,
This was theirs to do!

Never yet were pathways
By such heroes trod;
Never has a nation
Been so blest of God;
Never waved a banner
Over land so free;
Never yet were humans
Blest as blest are we!

Million Dollars

I've got a million dollars,
But of course it ain't in cash;
Got a little piece o' timber
Where there's maple, pine, an' ash.

I've got a sky that's studded
With a thousand stars at night,
An' that's painted like a picture
In the sunset's fadin' light.

I've got the great gray honkers
Headin' southward in the fall,
An' a heart that's all a-flutter
Ev'ry time I hear 'em call.

I've got the Christmas season,
With its hope an' joy an' cheer;
An' a springtime an' an autumn
Comin' to me ev'ry year.

I've got a hill for climbin'
When I want to be alone,
An' a thousand other blessings
That are all my very own.

An' nobody wants to buy 'em,
An' I'm glad enough to hold.
Yes, I've got a million dollars
But, you see, it ain't in gold!

A World of Friends

It's a wondrous world that we call our own,
With its granite mountains and peaks of stone,
With its gentle showers and sparkling dew,
And its bursting buds when the year is new.

It is painted crimson and brown and gold
With a magic brush when the year is old,
And is dazzling white when it's fast asleep
In the winter's arms, and the snow lies deep.

It's a world of flowers and skies and birds,
Of books and knowledge and lovely words,
A world that's fashioned for noble ends –
And best of all, it's a world of friends!

The Great Outside

Oh! Let me live in the great outside,
Where the hills are steep and the pastures wide,
Where the eagle soars in the far off blue,
And the fields are green when the year is new.

Yes, let me walk where the snow lies deep
In the winter woods when the world's asleep,
And feel the spell of the starlit night
In a world that's spotless and pure and white.

And when the autumn is brown and sere
And a glory comes with the dying year,
Then let me watch with a thrill untold
As nature paints with her brush of gold.

And then, good friend, when my day is done,
O bring me back where the setting sun
Lights up the hills at the eventide —
To rest, at last, in the great outside!

Values

If you had a million dollars,
Would the sun more brightly shine?
Would the grass be any greener
Or the weather be more fine?
Would the glory of October
Linger one more fleeting hour,
If you had a thousand millions
And a Caesar's awesome power?

Would the roses keep their petals
Any longer for your sake,
Or the snow hold greater wonders
In each oddly fashioned flake?
No, for good old Mother Nature
Takes no notice of your gold,
For her values have been measured
In another finer mold!

But if deep within your makeup
There abides a spark of love
For the good old earth beneath you,
Or the countless stars above,
Then you'll see a glory written
On the face of earth and sky
That great riches, fame and glory
Never, Never, Never buy!

Goodness of Man

There's a little bit of devil
In each man you chance to meet,
And the sands are ever shifting
'Neath his sometimes erring feet.

But it's well if you remember,
In each man and tree and clod,
In the sky and sea and mountain,
There's a little bit of God!

For the habit grows upon you –
See the devil in the man,
And you'll fail to see the glory
In the star-decked skies you scan.

You will feel the raging snowstorm
On a bitter winter night,
But you'll never know the beauty
Of a world all dressed in white.

Thorns and brambles – You will find them
On the mountain, ever nigh,
But you'll fail to feel the grandeur
Of its heights against the sky.

Look for God in man, however,
And you'll hear the songbirds sing;
See the glory and the beauty
God has placed in everything!

Childhood Neighbor

She was growing old and helpless
And her cheeks were wan and gray,
Eyes were dim and almost sightless,
And at last she slipped away.

Some there were who said 'twas better,
Since her step was weak and slow,
She could only be a burden;
It was better she should go.

But they never ate her cookies
As I used to when a lad,
And perhaps they never noticed
What a kindly way she had.

He who says that she was helpless,
"Now she's gone – 'Tis better so,"
Didn't know her just as I did
In the golden "Long Ago!"

The Kitchen Wall at Home

Tell me, stranger, as you painted,
Were there marks upon the wall,
As of someone who was growing,
And who wanted to be tall?

It was on this wall, each birthday
Dad would mark my height at last,
For each inch I'd grown in stature
In the year that then was past.

I recall my way of stretching
Till my joints would almost part,
For those marks were always something
Very special to my heart!

'Twas unwritten law that Mother,
When she painted, wouldn't dare
To erase those marks or touch them
Save with utmost love and care.

For you see this wall recorded
More than height to Dad and me,
It was more a dream or vision
Of the days that were to be!

And the hand of Time I'm certain,
On those marks would never fall.
Tell me, stranger, as you painted,
Were there marks upon the wall?

In Memory of Friends

I would like, today, to tell you
Of the friends we used to know,
Who were here and labored with us
Just a few short years ago.
Yes, I know, we are accustomed
To believe the years are long,
But the slightest observation
Proves that theory is wrong.

Years are short, but those old heroes
Made the most of every one,
Saw no day pass into darkness
With a duty left undone.
And we're better men and women
That they lived their little day,
For they left their mark upon us
Even though they couldn't stay.

So let's pause in admiration
As we hear the story told,
How they set the pattern for us
And how well they shaped the mold.
They were such good friendly people,
Ready with a word or smile,
And they lived and worked among us
Such a Little, Little While!

The Old Appetite

I'd like to be a boy again,
An' eat an' eat an' eat –
With everything a-tastin' good
If bitter, sour, or sweet.

The apples now don't seem to taste,
Nor look the way they did,
Back when I used to climb the tree
To get 'em as a kid.

I wish the berries nowadays
Was big an' ripe an' black,
An' sorta melted in your mouth,
The way they did years back.

These fancy walnuts that you buy,
From some far western grove,
Ain't like the hick'ry nuts we cracked
Around the kitchen stove!

An' shucks, a little measly dish
O' popcorn fills you so –
A heapin' dishpan wouldn't start
To do it long ago.

If I could, somehow, get a chance
To choose life's greatest treat,
I'd just be ten years old again –
An' eat, an' eat, an' eat!

Content

There are poets who discover,
In the leaders of their time,
Inspiration for great epics
And for noble thoughts in rhyme.

Others dream of bygone heroes,
Sing their praises to the last,
As they search the yellowed pages
Of a dim and mouldered past.

But I'd rather tell of forests,
And the pines that whisper there,
Of the leaves that turn to crimson
When the frost is in the air.

I would tell of brooks that babble,
And of birds that gaily sing,
Of the great gray geese of autumn,
And the flowers of the spring.

Other bards may tell the story
Of great leaders and their creeds,
Sing the everlasting glory
Of heroic men and deeds.

But if words of mine can picture
All the magic colors blent
In a gold and purple sunset,
Then my soul shall be content!

Disappearing Troubles

Have an awful lot o' troubles,
As I journey day by day,
Down the road we all must travel,
Down that long and lonely way;
Troubles that are always growin',
Worries that would gray your hair,
Problems that I just can't answer . . .
Till my brow is lined with care.

But when fields o' yellow stubble
Turn to green along in spring –
With the clover showin' through 'em,
After winter's had its fling –
Then my troubles sort o' vanish
As the red-winged blackbirds call,
An' my heart is almost burstin'
With the glory of it all!

An' I love to walk at evenin'
When the sun is sinkin' low,
Through the fields o' growin' clover,
Like my dad did long ago!
Yes, I got a lot o' troubles
But they mostly disappear,
When I'm walkin' in the meadows
In the springtime o' the year!

Homeland

Have you heard the coyotes howlin',
Seen the shiftin' desert sand?
Have you heard a rope go whistlin'
From a cowboy's skillful hand?

Then you've known the joy of livin'
In a world not made by man,
Where the human is a pygmy
Lost in nature's mighty plan!

Have you seen the moon a-risin'
Over miles of purple sage?
Heard the old north wind a-shriekin'
In the fury of its rage?

Then you've learned some things worth knowin'
In a way you'll not forget,
Of a mighty land unconquered,
Where the wild is master yet!

Have you felt the giant mountains
Cast their magic o'er the night?
Felt 'em closin' down around you
Like a blanket, snug and tight?

Then you'll never be contented
Cooped in four confinin' walls,
And the West will be your homeland
Till the final curtain falls!

Land

I'm the crest of the mountain, the shore of the sea,
And the bed of the river, they're all part of me.
I'm the source of your life, and the grass at your feet,
And the purple horizon where earth and sky meet!

I'm the home of your fathers, and your home at last;
I'm the hope of the future, the life of the past;
I'm the stern rocky cliff and the bright shining sand —
You must surely have guessed it, "I'm Land, I am Land!"

I must feed you and clothe you if you're to survive,
But to do it, I, too, must, in turn, stay alive.
So then, cleanse me with rivers, surround me with air
That are spotless and pure as when God put them there!